OKEY NWANGBURUKA, MD

Many Shades of Love
Copyright © 2024 by Okey Nwangburuka, MD

ISBN: 979-8895311233 (sc)
ISBN: 979-8895311240 (e)

All rights reserved. No part of this publication may be reproduced, distributed, or transmitted in any form or by any means, including photocopying, recording, or other electronic or mechanical methods, without the prior written permission of the publisher and/or the author, except in the case of brief quotations embodied in critical reviews and other noncommercial uses permitted by copyright law.

The views expressed in this book are solely those of the author and do not necessarily reflect the views of the publisher, and the publisher hereby disclaims any responsibility for them.

Writers' Branding
(877) 608-6550
www.writersbranding.com
media@writersbranding.com

Contents

About the Author vii
Why the Book? viii
Dedication ix

A. Green Lights

Love, predictably unpredictable 1
Love, peacefully 2
Love, no debt owed 4
Love, only you 5
Love, na you and me 6
Love, looking nyash killing goat 7
Love, living aligned 8
Love, liberating 10
Love, What Do I See? 11
Love, in dance 12
Love, how much? 13
Love, from town to country 14
Love, for bearing 15
Love, faithfully 16
Love, Dinner Date 17
Love, cruising together forever 18
Love, serendipitously 19
Love, throwback! 20
Love, Amazing 21

B. Red Hot Chemistry

Love, sweet surrender 23
Love, the scent of her!.. 24
Love, cut short 26
Love, conversating... 27
Love, better days ahead. 28
Love, another anticipation 29
Love, a dream come true 30
Love, a beautiful life 31
Love, unlimited! 32
Love, in winter 33

C. The Gray Dawn

Love, sixth day effect 35
Love, stupid! 37
Love, My Angels of Lies 39
Love, not loving yet 41
Love, womb whispers. 43
Love, what pain? 46
Love, to slay or not to slay! 48
Love, in due time... 49
Love, Homeless in America.. 50
Love, heartbreak! 51
What Do I See?... 52

D. Black Nights

No Solace Here..55
Love, what's left now? 56
Love, a story to be told! 59
Love, surviving covid! 61
Love stopped short 63
Love, seeing tomorrow 64
Love, prayerfully...65
Love, apply within 66
Love, WDIm..68
Love's Little Foxes..69

E. The White Lights of a New Morning

Not my Will..71
Love, womb whispers..72
Love, what pain? 75
Love, to slay or not to slay! 77
Love, thankfully..78
Love, tears, and joy!..80
Love, stronger and bigger 81
Love, Lest I Remember not...83
Love, sweet surrender...85
Love, one more chance 86
Love, IT WAS YOU 87
Love, such is life! 89

Epilogue

About the Author

Dr. Okey is a Dad, Physician, Entrepreneur, and Author.

He believes life can be built back better even after the trauma of decoupling. He doesn't believe the church should treat those whose love stories have shattered and fractured as pariahs in the body. God still restores when we come trusting only in the complete sacrifice of the Messiah.

Dr. Okey enjoys contemplative reflection, meditation, thinking, teaching, poetry, writing, and spending time with kids.

Why the Book?

In this attempt to highlight the beauty, pain, confusion, joy, and tears that come along with love, he expresses his views poignantly and hopes to inspire, educate, and warn lovers of the little foxes that negatively impact love for the long haul. He however encourages decoupled ex-lovers to live life to the fullest after their trauma.

Through different styles of poetry, he asserts that personal spiritual, intellectual, and emotional development, dependence on the Lord, and forgiveness are essential for healthy, comforting, and nurturing love relationships.

Dedication

To
All Lovers,
especially those who believe
in a Higher Power.

A. Green Lights

Love, predictably unpredictable

Amazing organic original virtues
bred in the south, drawn from loins of parents
influenced by sibs, education,
and training
Attractive, brave, cautious,
and daring, elegant, fabulous, generous and
mostly happy
Intriguing, jazzy, kempt and sincere in love
magnanimous, naughty, objective but not
puritan
queenly comportment, reticent, sassy, sexy
and troublesome sometimes and
understanding.
Vivacious, witty, externally down to earth
young but wise at matters of the heart
but what gives the zzz in our sacred buzz
is what I saw in my teen love
and see so much more now decades later.

Truly amazing, organic, original,
and all mine!

Love, peacefully

Come with me my lovely lady,
the feast is about to start,
and I need you by my side.
It's a come-just-as-you-are event
the venue is tripartite and flawless
In the hor d'oeuvres section, the way,
forgiveness, mercy, and cleansing are on the menu.
The inner sanctum, the truth,
has the best wines, gift bags,
separation, and dedication to true worship
wait my boo,
the best is yet to come
in the innermost court, the life,
we steppin' into new beat
and realms of glory
adoration unmatched musical outflow,
rivers crystal clear corridors of gold,
pillars of topaz and onyx.
Baby, my heart is already won over by

love and I yearn for you to meet the party host.
His name is the King of kings,
Prince of peace.

Love, no debt owed

He does not owe me,
I owe him every bit of me,
I can't question him,
he is not a man,
pre-existent one
only through looking upon his son,
Am I worth his mercy or grace?
He owes me not;
I am just asking for mercy.

Love, only you

What do I need?
Nothing but You.
Just you.
Not the blessings.
Just your presence.
Looking into your eyes
Fears falling off,
cast away by your love
doubts all dissolving
unbelief has no more space
just you and I,
all-day all-night
Be content,
my heart is all yours
you are mine; I am yours
no tabernacles,
the mansions are true
your perfect love has provided beyond measure.
Only your presence.
Your word. Just you.

Love, na you and me

'Though da whole world no be mine
but for my corner, na you be queen
my heart dey for gratitude riddim
say your love no consider my state
I sabi plenty wey for say romance v reality but
FBG na you be the real deal
na why I wan make u know say
na me and you together,
even for where u dey now, and forever.

Love, looking nyash killing goat

Wait o, my people I never talk finish
I wan talk about the finest chica nagbakam isi,
When I look am too much,
I fit call off work
Her waist dey make me go kolo
Like torotoro, she be specialist for to cook fresh gbonga fish, isi-ewu, intercontinental and even hen and cork peppersoup, bush meat, poundo, and ogbono.
Her grammar na out of this world, hia,
better sef say e dey down to earth
so e sabi wetin man need day and night
baba, gimme her or gimme no other
because this fine baby pikin na to die for.

Love, living aligned

Breathing but still gasping for air,
Feeding on choice meals but still hungry,
How I long for rivers of living water
And for bread, milk, and honey that's filling.
For all of you,
for deep ever-growing intimacy,
living maximally, living aligned.

Appreciating your love,
grateful for your patience.
Spending time with you,
learning to listen better.
Giving of all I have been blessed with cheerfully
Receiving thankfully without pride or shame.
Doing everything and anything that pleases you.
Living maximally, living aligned.

Your will, my command,
your wisdom my guide,
finding rest in your bosom,
peace reassured
Love ever kind,
not keeping record of insufficiency
for this journey
and beyond holding your hands
Praying for empathy, forgiveness,
gratitude, humility.
Loving you always, living aligned!

Love, liberating

Run, baby run
let us go over to the other side
with all our pains,
fears, and secrets,
with our failures, scars, and rejections.
The Master is waiting to lighten our load.
Just as we are,
guilty as charged,
hear the Master say,
our sins are forgiven
Our diseases healed,
no more condemnation
we are now at rest and peace
my fair lady!

Love, What Do I See?

I still see an amazing One
perfect in her imperfection,
kind and generous to a fault
struggling with insecurities
just like the rest of us
meeting all goals and deadlines
living in abundance of wealth
lacking neither joy nor good health
satisfied with all her heart's desires
fulfilling her life's mission and dreams
waking up rejoicing daily in stability.
I remain committed to my promise
to be there for the one who deserves more,
will not be deterred or discouraged
will keep praying and lifting you up
with the same passions our hearts ignited
many waters cannot quench the fire of love.

Love, in dance

It was not hip-hop, nor Afro-Caribbean stylee
this rhythm was strange,
entirely new to me
two-stepping or line dance would be easier
this tango is a communication in its own class
follow my lead,
mind your hold,
and your hips
I will keep my part,
and learn to trust my partner
this is commitment,
starting over when the rhythm is off
Can I go on with initial zeal,
or quit when rough?
More than passion is required,
discipline is an offer
I don't feel like going on
and giving up will be easier
so I thought
until my partner tapped my shoulder.
And love's commitment continued right back
afresh.

Love, how much?

How much do I love thee?
More than the bee and its honeycomb.
More than COVID's affection for China, Italy,
Germany, and USA combined.
So much more than the Tiv man loves his yam.
Bigger than Igbo man's love of money.
Stronger than Niger Deltans love Ogogoro.
Much more than the killing proclivities of ISIS,
Boko haram,
and all terrorist groups combined.
So much more than some pastors love tithes.
Stronger than the Yoruba man's tendency to
rake and brag.
More than some Naija politicians love looting
Naija funds.
And more than the so-called silent majority
loves Trump.
How much do I love thee?
More than any words can say.

Love, from town to country

Yarinya oma from City, Nmasinachi m,
we go dance to Aye, skelewu can wait.
We go sing collabo, dorrobucci no go enter
we go fly to limpopo and touch down Jerusalem
Beautiful Onyinye, we go taste
and chop our kudi for Baba go bless us pass
dami duro boy and Akon.
I go cover you from cold like Tiwa and
Flavour Okpekem,
I go dey look for you pass Caro n'ebaa.
We go raise altar because we know who we
be With Sinach,
and no matter the matter
I go duro for you as Baba dey on top our
matter.
So nothing go shake us, for onaga in our favor!

Love, for bearing

In my sight and all senses
no other woman would ever
compare to you,
your wit, intellect, bravado,
beauty, and guts
need you here
but understand the situation
so my yearning and longing I contain
hope maketh not ashamed,
for my love for you surpasses
that of the bee for its honeycomb.
I love you unconditionally, my lovely One.

Love, faithfully

My tears flow when I yearn for you when my soul thirsts for more of you triggered by pains and challenges
I know it's a cry and longing for you sometimes feel so alone and lonely even when I look back,
you've been my solace, Comforter, hope, and confidant. Known fully by you,
but still loves me
how great and faithful are your mercy and grace
Thank you.
For paying the ransom price for me for my freedom, joy, healing,
for drying my tears.

Love, Dinner Date

I know you got your little black dress ready But
tonight, the party reservation is for all whites
No wrinkles, spots,
hyper-pigmentation or wrinkles
No more pain, tears, illness, or weakness White
horses ready to convey us into royal presence
All guests robed in glorious colors, guest-gifts
prepared
Seven-course meals,
comparable to nothing on Old Ducks Our oils
full, hearts ready,
excited, waiting,
knowing we're complete and healthy in him,
knowing even as we are known.
Take my hand Ms. Amazing.
We are willing in the day of his power.

Love, cruising together forever

Hold my hand.
Let's gaze at the stars together
And hope for the future together
As we love super Kids together
And reach the world together.

With the truth we've shared together
Surrendering all we are together
To the one who's shown mercy
for the rest of our forever.

This story of us Deep, wide, long
Unmeasurable, unfathomable
Unrestricted, unlimited
flowing from the Fountain,
Finisher of our Faith.
Sweeter, better than flicks from Nollywood,
Hollywood, and Bollywood
This story of us,
E be like say na one in town.

Love, serendipitously

I could almost smell it
lay my hands on it
feel it but the closer I got
the more elusive it seemed.
Then serendipitously it happened
this was all so unusual really
that i may have to ask, humbly,
please make of me an honest person!

Love, throwback!

Tickles my fancy and fantasy
rocks my stars and my galaxy''''''''''
the only zero calorie sweetener in my tea''''''''
I dream about her in Samsung color
tolerates my awkward shyness and my goofiness''
my friends and I giggle about her beauty''''''''''
but she is the only one I adore.
Hope you don't mind the simplicity'' feeling like a schoolboy
writing his first true love
while the math class is going on!

Love, Amazing

Saw the best in me,
when others judged and discarded
restored and cleansed me
while they kept rehashing my past.
Told me everything would be alright
when they eagerly awaited my demise.
Love so amazing,
so pure and perfect invaded my world,
giving me hope and joy.
Love saw the best in me.

Love, heart skipping beats
While we talked today
You caused me to skip beats
Got me close to edge of pits
Where I was like melting ice cream
on your hot delicious palates.
Today while we talked
how my heart yearned for you.

B. Red Hot Chemistry

Love, sweet surrender

The influence of your presence,
gracious.
The sound of your covering,
undeniable.
The strength of your friendship,
overarching.
Hence to your love from the distance,
to your acceptance and nurture,
I totally,
and unashamedly surrender.
Knowing you bring me closer to
father's love, daily.

Love, the scent of her!

Lord, I am grateful you have forgiven me
Of all my iniquities, past, present, and future
And so, I love you with all of me
Surrendering all to you my King
Hence, I thank you for the blessing
And the comfort you have granted me
In and through this,
special awesome one Father,
you know this deep longing in me
Grant your son the favor of her fragrance
And of her scent by and around me always.
Not my will
but thine be done now and forever.

We met but...
At an age where a squeeze
of hands meant immensely
many cheesy lines sparked soul fires
A jealous friend always rushes
to come between soul-mates.

We met but...

Could not survive love's utopia
Cried eyes and hearts to numbness
Went with other options
that satisfied only partially
And pain's megaphone lessened loudness
but we never forgot a moment.

We met and…
This time it felt right
We set the past where it belonged
with trembling certainty started again
and this time there were full colors
In the sky and in our hearts.

We met and knew it felt right.
Affirmed to us it was time.
The right time to try again.
So happy we met again.

Love, cut short

So wrong about being right this time
Even though she was an answer from above
the joy and gladness were always short-lived
Accusations, finger-pointing, blaming
Limited time being spent together, she said
One day a hero,
the next a problem lover
Are these what are called red flags later?

The stress of the yo-yo was not worth it
No laughter, no depth of conversation
Said I love you much, almost to exhaustion
would come pleading after vitriolic outbursts
Oh, what fatal attraction might this become
Better to respect her decision now,
Had offered, but she refused over and over,
probably wanted control of when and how
the affair comes to an end?

Love, conversating

I am totally yielded,
He is Master,
I am son
whatever he wishes,
whatever he desires
I am yielded,
no questions asked
Glad only to dwell in his presence.
I am totally yours, Master.

Love, better days ahead.

New starts, brighter hopes,
bigger dreams.
Courage, letting go,
looking past shattered dreams.
Now I know,
now I see,
the promises, the pains
Tomorrow holds much more,
much more gains.
All things meshing together,
not just for my good
but for life's bests
denied by events fore and odd.
New starts, brighter hopes,
bigger dreams
Now mine,
with all of me
and mine in his hands.

Love, another anticipation

Fading memories and mixed emotions
the sky was darkening in blunted blues
the stars appeared to be in jubilation
As angels ascended and descended above
but that was decades ago
when Lagos came to Maiduguri
and birthed reconnection.
Our lips locked, mouths melted, tongues tangled!
We sang Hallelujah
and wished it would be forever.
Time has passed, much newness for celebrations
and some tears shed, all in love.
I now wonder about another long kiss
but might it be a brotherly kiss
or something better
I am curious, my muscles!
But this longing still fills my soul!

Love, a dream come true

It was a dream, but not just.
You were on your feet,
even if still a lil ill.
I scaled the walls to be with you
And could show a bit of what this heart feels.
You held my hand
and we took a short walk
Sat on the garden seat
just outside the house.
And then you held my head in your hands
Kissing me is only possible in anoda life.
You lit a million fires in me
Sparks of lightning so unreal.
Your eyes said enough and then I knew
None else could ever take the place
Of this king in my heart.

Love, a beautiful life

The curveballs or celebrations?

The things we feared that came upon us?

The deep and secret things

that seem to influence our paths? Despite all, we have cause to give thanks for the breath of life

for the unseen battles he won for us

for the joys of friendship, romance, and love for the special moments

we will share together, knowing

life is a gift

to be lived in abundance. Life is beautiful.

What else can we compare it with?

Love, unlimited!

Cravings for more than a touch
longing for encounters beyond words
knowing
there remains no space for other gods
in new realms without limits
and impossible not a dictionary word
conduit, flowing with destiny-changing love
felt through an embrace,
a touch, a whisper a movement,
trusting the unknown
resting assured when tomorrow comes
there will be laughter,
and joy unspeakable
Hence, I am no longer afraid
to step out in love.
Sponsored by mercy, grace,
and amazing beauty.

Love, in winter

The voice was on the other side of the wall
The wall seems divisive and unclimbable
not unlike the Southern Border Trump
till I strain my heart to get close to the flow
but voices in my head are in a noisy ball
with DJ scratching and mixing "Atlantic Starr"
leaving me dazed to dance or to run
I give in, I give up.
I begin to gyrate with her
drawing so close
but still on the other side of the wall.

C. The Gray Dawn

Love, sixth day effect

It was now six days and more
of torturous sheer silence
Silenced unexplained,
felt discarded,
Dispensable and demeaned
but no worries,
so when I woke up
in the early predawn hour to
my ambient silence,
I knelt in my heart
I woke up and wept and wailed silently.

It was not because of hindering prison
walls
nor the affliction, pain, or the silence
Lord,
maybe I had missed the mark again
Maybe I should have waited,
listened more
As I wept,
I told Master I was sorry,

and sought Mercy
Grace made it possible,
I was cleansed, restored
I was gratefully relieved,
I felt a fresh refreshing
Different from when I woke up and wept.

Soon afterward, not up to an hour later
The silence was broken,
and I received the message
From the other prison
where there was isolation,
All I could think of
was a wish to cross over
make eye contact,
and chop knuckles in support
but since that was not possible for now
I prayed,
knowing all things would turn out well.
I rested.
It no longer mattered that I had woken earlier,
woken up to silence, and had wept!

Love, stupid!

Some unravel so quickly
others surprisingly after many years
the therapists and wiser ones have their
theories
Preachers, rabbis, and scientists are not left out.
Who has the mysterious secret to success
then?

How costly and badly so many are hurt!
Three-point sermons and evidence-based facts
offer no comfort, meaning, or hope.
The bitterness can be so tangible,
wroth in vengeance and wrath,
friends usually forsake,
looking into keeping theirs safe
and try not to be over-involved.
others come vulture-like advantage to take

Young offspring are left so confused
they rebel but it was not so
at the beginning.

High hopes, perpetual promises,
love seemingly unconquerable
and it all comes crashing,
fault or no-fault status
they could not imagine themselves in
the cold court
when they were rocking to the DJ's
music in reception.

Words, actions, lusts so unforgivable?
Pain and hurt so deep definitely!
Who can save us from ourselves?
More than one out of two affected and
the vicious cycle continues
when kids are badly affected
and not helped
no surprise that
since all hearts yearn for love
the eternal flowing milk of hope
causes for second, third, and more
attempts.
Love, really?

Love, My Angels of Lies

Perfection impersonated,
loveliest liars in the Land
Smooth deception, words of half-truth
Designed to invoke sympathy
for victim Angel,
To tear down, malign,
and document manufactured innocence.

But Jehovah is documenting the wickedness
being told:
He would not help you
if you were in his shoes
Does not care about the children,
and calls him a destroyer of hope
wasteful, unfaithful, and lascivious monster
Never defended or did anything good for them
Sided with back-stabbers
and testified
he was a liar,
sowed seeds of discord
among his friends and family

Yet pretends to be seeking peace.

May their honor be turned to dishonor
May their favor become disfavor
As every Judas hangs himself
Their turn is around the corner
As Jehovah exposes and takes vengeance
On my mocking and scorning,
conniving Angels of Lies.

Love, not loving yet

Not a Slave of Fear or Doubt
sounds like the popular song title
but I hear the music of faith
as I look back over two decades
as I consider our four miracles
still feel the punch of betrayal
now fighting for equity brazenly
and I look up with gratitude
I am at least still here to care for you!

Anywhere but here,
no room left in the inn
to be accused of oddities
not qualified to be informed of your plans
and dreams
yet fingers, pointing fingers once again,
accuse me of not sharing,
even though I talk about life and death with you
I do not want to be responsible for the choices
you make without discussion or consultation
Is there still a place called it for us?
Is there any better there than the journey so

far?
If I could have seen this new year from last year, would I have wished away any events or experiences?
Would I be questioning God as to why me?
Or would I be wallowing or joying in what is?
Would I pray away negative people, places, or processes?
Would I have the state of fortitude to pick and choose what happens?

I think not, for every person, place, and process was making for my good.
Every event designed to help me grow, to love.
To be patient, to give thanks in all things.
To teach me to war, and that my flight is in my fight.
So now I am thankful for all the people, and places,
for he allowed every piece in place to help maximize my life
and love my way to your heart.
Love always trusts and can last forever.

Love, womb whispers.

Wisdom calls out,
but often my eyes blind my ears,
making it difficult
to discern the wheat or the tare!
Recognition during incubation,
e'en before it's late
Oh sounds of life, reveal and direct my heart.
Teach me to see the Invisibles
that my heart's open to,
Pray, enlighten me womb whispers.

Listen for the sound of honor, even when angry,
Watch for patience and level of priority,
for the desire to uplift
and encouragement to serve,
Respect for you, family and friends, spirituality?
Love to give, proud of your success, not envious?
Womb whispers are always present.
Slow to anger, fast to forgive,

enjoying even your silence.
communicating in your love languages,
and sharing dreams.
Not given to habits you surely can't stand,
worthy of honor.
May not have much materially now,
but full of goals and drive.
Above all, understanding that
this marathon is about destiny
Not lovey-dovey emotions,
growing in vertical relations.
Womb whispers always for discerning hearts.

If after you have done all,
and center falls apart,
After you have fought for the relationship,
not your partner,
after all interventions appear to fail,
even time apart,
when it seems you can't breathe
although taking in air,
Cry if you must,
engage your close circuit circle, look up.

One day you will recall
there's first John and second John!
Womb whispers now life can still go
on, actually better!

Love, what pain?

Which pain, this or that?
That which threatens my faith?
Or the force that draws me to Father?
Which pain? Of brokenness or journey?
Of dreams slowed and perspectives challenged?
Or should I ask what pain?
That suffered in silence every moment?
Could it be that which draws tears unexplainable?
Of physiological, emotional, or spiritual roots?
How can I forget that from new growth, pruning has unknowingly brought out its beauty?

What pain?
Knowing this one thing: the joy to come
will overcompensate for all endured
then I am confident, neither in me nor men.
You point to limitations, failures, and tears
May I redirect you to my inside man

Holding on, believing,
resting on his assurances
Pain? So what?
Part of the journey to glory.
Yes, which pain?
What pain?
Joy and hope have triumphed in this love race.

Love, to slay or not to slay!

If it were too difficult for him,
he would have told me.
But he didn't, because it's not.
So, I know I can trust him.
I can. I will.
Even if he slays me,
yet will I hang my all on him!

How time flies
it's been seven years already,
years of famine and loss
of pain and degeneration
but Chi Ukwum loved still
despite the unworthiness
his mercy said yes, yes.
My strength failed me
some friends and family MIA
body mangled; spirit preserved
Love provided, no resources lacked
how time flies, how time flies.
And I remain thankful for your love!
My consolation, my Light, my love

Love, in due time.

If it were not so,
He would have said so.
I can be confident
with him, nothing is difficult he has heard
and love will manifest in due season.
Love that never fails, comfort and peace you give have kept me.
I am grateful, eternally!

Love, Homeless in America

Did not see the spiral
Was fighting for life
Clinging unto strands of hope
oblivious to the bills partially paid
Since my discharge from the hospital.
Loved ones didn't want me to know how low
my credit score had gotten
So tough getting into apartment
but the pastor
and an angel came to the rescue
Who knows the rains,
the winter cold,
the street
would have swallowed me up!

Love, heartbreak!

No beautiful way to say it
no glamorous style to give space
must be a case of two different worlds
colliding with many collaterals unanticipated
but what must be
maybe should not be bound
would be foolish to get entangled
in a worse mess
No, you have done nothing wrong,
and I am sorry
phrases often used without depth or character,
so, so long baby,
no beautiful way to say it
no glamorous way to end it,
we both hurt
but we both are from worlds so apart and different,
it's better now than later,
takes nothing away
from a great gal, a lovely lady, with heart and issues.
So, goodbye and good night, my fair lady.

What Do I See?

I still see an amazing One,
perfect in her imperfection,
kind and generous to a fault
struggling with insecurities,
just like the rest of us,
meeting all goals and deadlines
living in abundance of wealth,
lacking neither joy nor good health
satisfied with all her heart's desires
fulfilling her life's mission and dreams
waking up rejoicing daily in stability.

I remain committed to my promise
to be there for the one who deserves more will
not be deterred or discouraged
will keep praying and lifting you up
with the same passions our hearts ignited
many waters cannot quench the fire of love.

Never saw or squeezed the cylindrical cap
Not out of a lack of desire or demand

but because we wanted not to defile
a tad of that which friendship had in trust wrought
Now after much wisdom sought and bought
Through hard and easy knocks, prayers, and thought
Much conversation and gracious communication
I have been given permission to use imagination
to describe the supple ridged encircling passage with its perfect, dark chocolate magnetic cap
A coalition of tender responsive sensory innervation
which I have learned remains consecrated twins
Abiding and awaiting the end of waiting time.
Lord, cleft for me a place upon that special Soul!

D. Black Nights

No Solace Here.

No more tears left
Not even crying in the rain
Tear ducts filled with blood
Unable to drip down
The one I held so dearly,
ate and drank with,
depended upon
has pierced my sides over and over.

My heart so heavy from the hemorrhage
Simply to the Cross I now cling
This poisoned arrow is no mere distraction
Shafted by your very own person
This is no happy place,
No raven-delivered comforts here,
But I will ask no questions in my foolishness
Come, Lord, come and deliver me
I need You, only You, only You now.

Love, what's left now?

The burning questions still linger
The hollow helplessness getting number
Insomnia now an enduring nightly partner
No tears left not even when I pray
It bumbles out Lord,
the pain is searingly wicked
But we do not question,
only that you will surrender.
Memorable memories!
More memories!
Fewer imaginations!

Wrestling with the sheer torture
of all the whys
Losing appetite and weight
while receiving guests
Hearing comforting
and encouraging words mostly.
I was nudged ever so gently.
I almost asked aloud "What are you saying?"
with feelings of self-pity
and the still small voice was persistent

and prickly " What's left now?
Count what tangibles are left! "
Memories, memories, overflood my
mourning soul.

I retreat to a solitary corner
I lifted my itchy eyes and looked up
Wishing for whispering angelic help
Then I realized I still had some cause
to be thankful and grateful for.
Memories! Memories! Pleasant, painful!

Mercy, with its access to grace.
Grace, that opens doors of needful help.

Wife, mom, kids, sibs, in-laws, friends,
businesses!
His presence, his promises, and assurances
of love.
Though the aches remain and painfully so,
I am still looking up to the hills from this
valley.
Surprisingly, the tears began to flow afresh

This time I was overwhelmed
by my father's love!
Memories, memories.
More imagination in Light!

Love, a story to be told!

This is a story
a story that must be told
A testimony of His goodness when
they gave us no hope
but rather gave up on us.

My sisters didn't back out,
stood by me in the darkest hours
fought in every way to keep me alive
friends and some family gave up
but not these strong women

Interesting that those who said
Prayers being prayed were wasted
now come,
not for reconciliation
but to insinuate and malign
while unknowingly showing their
greed
no anger or hurt, no malice or
grudge

just a reminder of how life
changes sometimes.

But the story must be told,
the story of his sustenance
the testimony of his healing
the tale of goodness and mercy.

Yes, the story must be told.

Love, surviving covid!

Life slipping away without warning,
heart rate angrily slowing down the depths
to a place of isolation and desolation
mind and soul unquestionably following
Leftover feelings numbing to previous realities!

All the questions running around
my drained brain,
my two little queens,
one yet to be held,
Yet to be nurtured, succored, or warmly loved.
No strength left for tears in this cubicle
I could barely hear the sudden silence
of those who had continued beyond me
to the other side,
no strength to ponder
why those with me wouldn't tell
Or touch or talk to me,
though their love abounds!

And this thing helping me breathe,
medicine through my veins.

Is this the spelling of Death?
Mercy made way for grace,
Grace accessed Love
and the Trinity said, "Not yet",
so much left to be done for my kingdom.
The Substitution and Advocate pleaded my case,
producing pleas for strong causes.
And the righteous judge dismissed all charges.
Recall was stopped by love, mercy, and grace.

When I came to,
I was asked what love is.
Love?
It's surviving the cold cruel clutches of covid!

Love stopped short

We don't even talk anymore
not that we were very disclosing
before your attorney painted me a demon,
they say she is doing her job.
I read them and wonder,
truly wonder if you believe this,
why did you not unhitch and wait till
my worst crisis to put pressure?

Never for a second did I think
our city-to-city-to-village experiences
would end this way!

Albeit, I am sorry for all things gone wrong
and thankful for all the good, bad,
and ugly!

Love, seeing tomorrow

If I could see tomorrow,
would I change its course?
Would I know enough about impact
to follow through?
Would I be strong enough
to let what shall be to be?
Would I be courageous enough
to see the bad and their timings?
would the good still feel good
when I get there?

Pondering, wondering,
and questioning life, love?
Higher purpose, worship, altruism,
at the end of meaning?
Why am I here?
What is it all about!?
Where shall my end be?
Please teach me pain! Please teach me joy!
If I could see tomorrow, then what?

Love, prayerfully

Not sure what's going on
the stress and heartache,
the fears and tension
but it stops your flow,
impacts your attention
and here I sit,
feeling helpless and forlorn
when suddenly I realize he has your back
and all he loves and cares so much about you
that he would not withhold from you
anything fun
he will fight your battles
and take away your burden
now I can close my eyes
and pray for my lovely one,
knowing the one who has you in his palms,
strong will renew his faithfulness,
come this dawn,
just for you,
only for and always for my pretty one.

Love, apply within

Sometimes felt like brotherly affection
or just as an erotic connection.
Some say it is a deity-like commitment
Yet others describe a quality friendship.
What beautiful feelings that come with it,
Or is it a choice decision,
or a gift from above?
Love, who art thou?

The heart skips beats,
butterflies in the stomach.
Knocking knees and a tendency to project,
and identify and minimize deficits
so to magnify
cleaving of hearts,
mating of souls,
kiss of hands.
Why does something beautiful go south at times?
Some think it can be bought, but can you be taught?

Love, how are you identified,
for a heart's eternity?

A voice says, listen to your heart
and not your mind
Another reminds me,
feelings come and go,
not reliable.
Family backgrounds,
compatibility concerns,
Sociocultural issues,
spirituality,
it gets complicated
Love, who art thou?
Where are you?
How right?
And Love replied silently.
I am that I am, apply within.
The Compass with you,
the road's rough,
I will guide you!

Love, WDIm.

An unending list of challenges,
Difficulties unceasing, tearing us apart
So many willing to render advice unsolicited
Others hanging in our flanks mocking
Deceivers pretending to cheer but, yes but
Only console in our pain, never joyful in our joy
A few faithful keep their distance with encouragement
Wasn't like this after we first got together.
Where did we let us drift apart?
Where did we go wrong?
Long list of challenges,
but what does it matter?
If we can forgive, and commit to trying again?
What does it matter if we value all that we had?
What does it matter if we can say I am sorry?
Or just start holding hands again, Babe?
What does it matter?

Love's Little Foxes.

Not communicating truthfully

Dishonoring others in ways shameful

Disregarding making time for each other

Fighting one another rather than for union

Fighting unfairly but using shared secrets

Not resolving extended family matters

Sex, sex, sex, and sex!

Money, money, money, and money!

What of personal development in all spheres?

Little foxes, eating at our tender roots.

E. The White Lights of a New Morning

Not my Will

May thy Kingdom come
May thy will be done!
How now vain,
Meaningless,
erstwhile confessions,
determinations

Father, whatever you will
Whatsoever you desire
Whatever you want from me
Your sovereignty, not my will.

Love, womb whispers.

Wisdom calls out,
but often my eyes blind my ears,
making it difficult
to discern the wheat or the tare!
Recognition during incubation,
e'en before it's late
Oh sounds of life, reveal and direct my heart.
Teach me to see the Invisibles
that my heart's open to,
Pray, enlighten me womb whispers.

Listen for the sound of honor, even when angry,
Watch for patience and level of priority,
for the desire to uplift
and encouragement to serve,
Respect for you, family and friends, spirituality?
Love to give, proud of your success, not envious?
Womb whispers are always present.
Slow to anger, fast to forgive,

enjoying even your silence.
communicating in your love languages,
and sharing dreams.
Not given to habits you surely can't stand,
worthy of honor.
May not have much materially now,
but full of goals and drive.
Above all, understanding that
this marathon is about destiny
Not lovey-dovey emotions,
growing in vertical relations.
Womb whispers always for discerning hearts.

If after you have done all,
and center falls apart,
After you have fought for the relationship,
not your partner,
after all interventions appear to fail,
even time apart,
when it seems you can't breathe
although taking in air,
Cry if you must,
engage your close circuit circle, look up.

One day you will recall
there's first John and second John!
Womb whispers now life can still go
on, actually better!

Love, what pain?

Which pain, this or that?
That which threatens my faith?
Or the force that draws me to Father?
Which pain? Of brokenness or journey?
Of dreams slowed and perspectives challenged?
Or should I ask what pain?
That suffered in silence every moment?
Could it be that which draws tears unexplainable?
Of physiological, emotional, or spiritual roots?
How can I forget that from new growth, pruning has unknowingly brought out its beauty?

What pain?
Knowing this one thing: the joy to come
will overcompensate for all endured
then I am confident, neither in me nor men.
You point to limitations, failures, and tears
May I redirect you to my inside man

Holding on, believing,
resting on his assurances
Pain? So what?
Part of the journey to glory.
Yes, which pain?
What pain?
Joy and hope have triumphed in this love race.

Love, to slay or not to slay!

If it were too difficult for him,
he would have told me.
But he didn't, because it's not.
So, I know I can trust him.
I can. I will.
Even if he slays me,
yet will I hang my all on him!

How time flies
it's been seven years already,
years of famine and loss
of pain and degeneration
but Chi Ukwum loved still
despite the unworthiness
his mercy said yes, yes.
My strength failed me
some friends and family MIA
body mangled; spirit preserved
Love provided, no resources lacked
how time flies, how time flies.
And I remain thankful for your love!
My consolation, my Light, my love

Love, thankfully

For the breath of life,
and daily bread
for victories seen,
and battles won unseen,
for foes crushed
and angels of lies defeated,
for deliverance from shame,
and humiliation
shielding me from their wicked plans,
in mercy
shattering their evil expectations,
your favor
giving your angels charge over me,
I leap
now beyond the beautiful gate,
not on the roof
no longer waiting for angel-stirred pool
I am taking leave of this bed,
singing into the sunshine,
the shame gone, accusing tongues
condemned

I look up and hear I am
forgiven, made whole
a billion tongues of mine
cannot thank you enough
I simply offer the sacrifice
of my praise and love
worshiping thankfully.

Love, tears, and joy!

I cry not for how I feel
I cry because I am beckoning
to the heavens
I cry for mercy, for grace,
and not because I feel like being treated like a dog
if you must know ml,
for symptoms beyond my control!
I wish I didn't have to depend on others
I cry not because I need others, I do!
But not being able to do shit for myself!
What more can I say? I cry sometimes-
Weeping only briefly,
for joy comes again soon!

Love, stronger and bigger

Call it what you wish,
Challenge or crisis, cancer, or even calamity!
Disease, death-beckoning dire straits, or demons.
Disappointments, financial hardships, pain seen unseen,
I am bigger and stronger than them all!

Situations that defy all human solution,
Circumstances that place persons between rocks,
Strife, backbiting friends, disloyalty and betrayal,
Embarrassments, shame, guilt, doubt, unbelief,
I am bigger and stronger than them all!

Altars and covens, strongmen and women,
Witches and wizards, agents of hell and hades,
Things existing or yet to be unfolded,
Envious enemies against progress and prosperity,
I am bigger and stronger than them all!

Situations that defy all human solutions.
Rejections, circumstances that place persons between rocks.
Hollow emptiness,
hopelessness,
and helplessness
Embarrassments, shame, guilt, doubt, unbelief,
I am bigger and stronger than them all!

Altars and covens, strongmen and women,
Witches and wizards, agents of hell and hades,
Political juggernauts wielding power negatively
Death of family, friend, mentor, and even child.
I am bigger and stronger than them all.

Disfavor, things past, present, and future
Occultic encumbrances, wickedness of all sorts
Procrastination,
bad, broken, and shattered relationships
I am stronger and bigger than them all.
All because the greatest One is in me.
-

Love, Lest I Remember not

Lost mobility,
but still alive
Not six feet under,
still here for fab four.
Second chance from above,
divine destiny to fulfill
Lost many friends,
now with faithful few
lost speech,
yet able to communicate
feel unworthy and confused,
mercy ever-present.
Pained by family fractured,
joyful when kids come.
Unable to work,
Love providing needed care
On bed day and night,
looking up and no bed sores
loving sisters sacrificing,
destiny helpers provided,
prayer warriors unceasing,
forgiveness received,

breathing lungs affected,
twin breather vent availed
Suctioning and secretions and body pains,
not drowned
legal difficulties abounding,
surmounted by His justice
immobile and dependent,
yet faculties preserved
so much to be thankful for,
lest I remember not.

Love, sweet surrender.

The influence of your presence,
gracious.
The sound of your covering,
undeniable.
The strength of your friendship,
over-arching.
Hence to your love
from the distance,
to your acceptance and nurture,
-I totally, and unashamedly surrender.
Knowing you bring me closer
to my father's love, daily.

Love, one more chance

To say and to show how truly sorry I am.
To do the things I left undone
And to atone for things wrongly done.
To serve you and to please you,
Love I pray for a chance more.

How oft I had made the same mistakes,
Each time taking your forgiveness for granted
But, here I am again, pleading for mercy
So, I can call you your beautiful names, Adore,
magnify, and just bask in our koinonia.
Love, I pray for just a chance more.

You are the strength of my life,
the One always dependable,
reliable, and gracious,
thy loving-kindness is better than life itself.
I just want to give my utmost for you to deserve it!
Love, just one more chance to be all yours!
Just one more chance, love I pray.

Love, IT WAS YOU

I dreamed he would be my friend We would talk and laugh
We would cry and fight over the silliest things,
I should have known It was you.

The beautiful moments shared in prayer,
in just being
So long ago when so young.
Why did I not know
it was you?

A time of innocence, of pure joy,
of peacefulness and much support,
And I did not know It was you.

You gave the friendship I needed,
the one I still crave
You listened and spoke
And wanted to hear me pray.
It was you

My handheld in encouragement
A prayer, a sigh,
A walk in the park
Dreams spoken of
A hug, a kiss
It was you.

Then innocence was lost
and fear took its place
Yet with every twinge of heart
and memories of that one time.
That moment of forever.
It was you.

And now time and space and pain
and uncertainty set us apart
I'd give anything to know back then,
that It was you.

Love, such is life!

Inescapable stuff of life.
The marrow between spirit, soul, and body.
Minimized by some.
Exaggerated by others.
Important and unignorable,
no matter class, race, creed, wealth, or
education.
Born as if into the race of going through
Freudian, Maslowian, or Eriksonian stages.
Inescapable and undeniable stuff of real life.
Disease, conquests, discoveries, families or not
Economic imbalances,
rich versus poor
well versus unwell,
outspoken versus voiceless
Wars and clashes and friction,
and even religion.
Inescapable and undeniable stuff of life.

Some in tears others jubilating
but through it all the lowest common
denominator

for male, female boy, girl, LGBTIQQ, pansexual, or whichever class
No one knows how and when the end comes.
Sadly, excuse the suicidal para-suicidal cohort!
No comfort from fame, name, riches, connections
What's the purpose of it all?
Philosophers' field day!
Mergers, acquisitions, collaborations, forced sales?
Losses, gains, break-evens, dissatisfactions, fractures,
Ambitions, dreams, pursuits, winnings, vows, oaths, Competitions, failures, doubts, fears.
Real tangible undeniable stuff of life.

Minimizing it to purpose,
spirituality can't cut it
Conquering outer space and other races do not!
Deaths, births, schools, passages
tearful goodbyes, joyous welcomes, indifferent expressions

Volume of books,
it is in there for each of us
Not astrology
nor books shrouded in mystery
thanks to the one existing before time and creation
The one worthy to open the volume specifics
we need him for life's undeniable
but mostly unimportant and the very few stuff that matters.

Epilogue

Thanks for sharing this space with me. I hope you were able to identify with some of the emotions and cognition. Truth be told, we all need quality meaningful relationships, fueled by the love that we yearn for! If this has been your experience, we rejoice with you.

But if you have been dealt a bad hand, I want to assure you there's hope. The One who created you for a fulfilling love relationship hasn't given up on you. He is here right now to fill that vacuum in your heart.

If you are interested in letting him hold your hand and give you a new start, please take a minute and repeat this prayer in your heart!

"Lord Jesus, forgive me my sins. I believe you died for me. I confess you are my lord and savior. Come and take your rightful place in my life. Fill me with the holy spirit to guide me. Thanks for writing my name in your book of life.

Thank you, Lord."

www.ingramcontent.com/pod-product-compliance
Lightning Source LLC
LaVergne TN
LVHW041535070526
838199LV00046B/1679